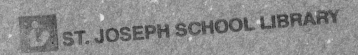

CORAL REEF

Michael George

CREATIVE EDUCATION

Designed by Rita Marshall
with the help of Thomas Lawton

© 1992 Creative Education, Inc.
123 South Broad Street,
Mankato, Minnesota 56001

Photo research by Kathleen Reidy

Photography by Peter Arnold,
Richard Grigg, David Hall,
Jeffrey L. Rotman, Franklin Viola,
Waterhouse, and Anne Wertheim

Library of Congress
Cataloging-in-Publication Data

George, Michael, 1964–
The coral reef / by Michael George.
     p.   cm.
Summary: Examines the formation
of coral reefs and the kinds of
animals that live there.
ISBN 0-88682-430-3
1. Coral reef fauna—Juvenile
literature.   2. Corals—Juvenile
literature.   [1. Coral reef biology.
2. Coral reef ecology.   3. Ecology.]
I. Title.   91-10885
QL125.G46   1991   CIP
574.5' 26367—dc20   AC

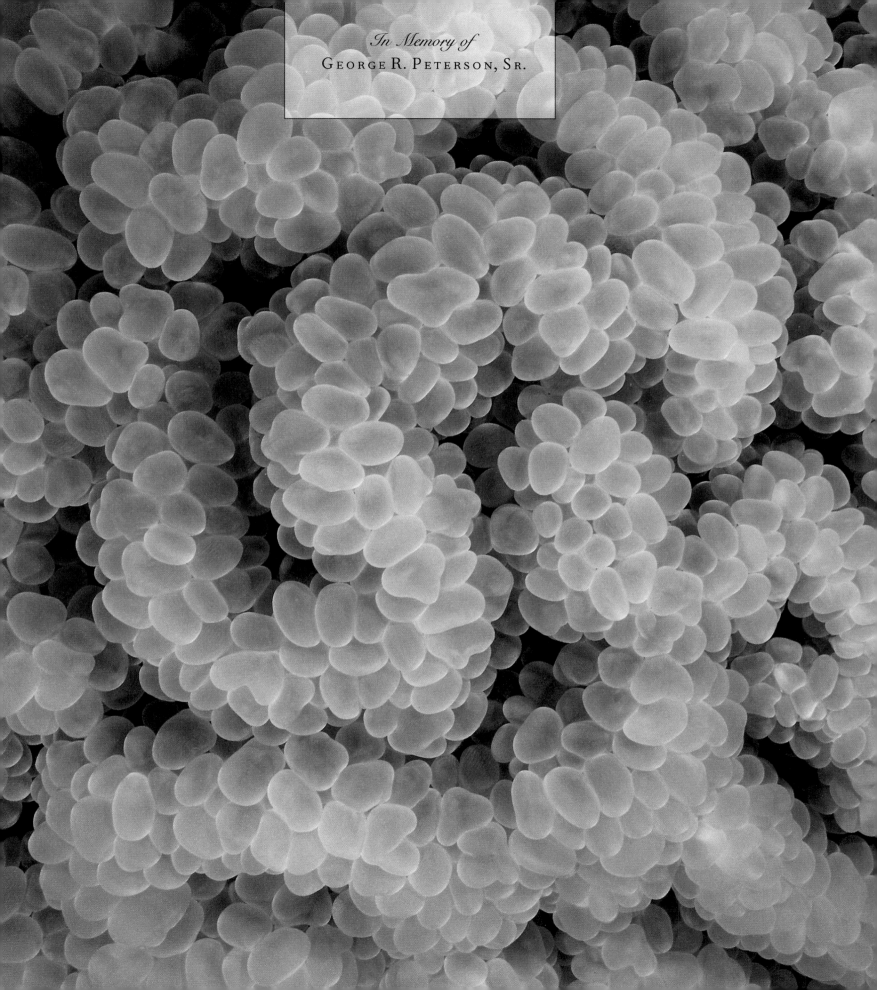

Human beings are designed for life on land. As a result, many of us are somewhat biased. We feel that the Earth's continents and islands are the most comfortable and beautiful places to live. But dry land is the exception on the Earth—most of our planet is covered by water. The Earth's blanket of water hides a world filled with unfamiliar sights, sounds, and beauty.

The ocean.

One of the most fascinating habitats beneath the ocean's surface is the *Coral Reef*. Located in warm, shallow seas, coral reefs are enormous, rocklike structures that are inhabited by unfamiliar forms of life. Underwater channels, crevices, and caves provide hiding places for eels and sharks, octopuses and snails, odd-looking fish, and more microscopic organisms than you could ever count. The coral reef is one of the most amazing collections of life in the world.

A coral reef is not formed in the same way that continents or islands are formed. Unlike mountains, deserts, and most other natural landscapes, it does not even consist of rocks and soil. Instead, it is a huge city built by tiny animals called *Coral Polyps*.

A coral reef.

The construction of a coral reef is begun by a single coral polyp. Early in life, immature polyps, called *Planulae,* drift freely through the ocean. Planulae are tiny, vulnerable animals; many are eaten by other sea creatures before they reach adulthood. Those that survive settle on the seafloor in shallow water. Here, the planulae develop into adult coral polyps.

Compared to more familiar creatures such as dogs or humans, coral polyps are very simple animals. Even after they are fully grown, most coral polyps are smaller than your fingernail. They do not have arms, legs, or even eyes. A polyp's body looks like a tiny tube made out of jelly. The polyp's mouth is located at the top of the tube. It is surrounded by small, poisonous tentacles.

Page 10: Soft coral polyps.
Page 11: Hard coral polyps.

Although reef-building polyps are animals, they cannot move around like fish, birds, or humans. The lower half of the polyp's body is covered by a hard, limestone skeleton that cements the polyp to the seafloor. Known as *Stony Corals,* these polyps sacrifice mobility for security. When disturbed, the soft-bodied polyp ducks into its rocklike home.

During the day, most kinds of stony corals hide inside their protective shelters. The polyps emerge at dusk, as the sun sets and the sky grows dark. With their tentacles swaying in the water, the polyps search for food.

Adult polyps feed on tiny, immature sea animals such as shrimps, crabs, and fish. When one of these organisms brushes against a polyp's tentacles, the tentacles stun it with a dose of poison. The tentacles then sweep the victim into the polyp's mouth and the polyp digests its tiny meal.

Staghorn coral branches.

Supplied with abundant food and suitable living conditions, a coral polyp soon begins to reproduce, forming other polyps that will share its living space. Through a process called *Budding,* new polyps appear on the body of the original polyp. Each new polyp builds its own limestone shelter attached to that of its parent.

Stony coral polyps.

Ever so slowly, coral polyps multiply until they create enormous *Coral Colonies.* Some colonies contain millions of individual polyps. The shape of a colony depends on the species of coral. Some colonies look like big boulders, while others grow in the shape of tree branches or deer antlers. Still other colonies resemble large plates or shelves. There are even colonies that have ridges and creases like those of a human brain.

Stony coral.

Over many years, coral colonies establish themselves, grow into their characteristic shapes, and eventually die. Even after a colony dies, however, the polyps' hard limestone shelters remain. Given enough time, a new coral colony establishes itself upon the durable skeletons of its ancestors. Thus, over many hundreds of years, countless generations of polyps slowly produce a jumble of limestone boulders, branches, and shelves —a coral reef.

Australia's Great Barrier Reef.
Inset: Patterns of growth.

19

Coral reefs do not arise just anywhere beneath the ocean's surface. In order to develop properly, coral polyps have certain requirements. Reef-building polyps need sunlight to survive, so they cannot live in deep, dark ocean water. They also need warm water, abundant food, and fixed levels of salt and oxygen. The only places where all these conditions are met are in tropical regions of the Earth. As a result, living coral reefs are found only in clear, shallow water near the Earth's equator.

A coral island off Belize.

Because reef-building polyps must live in shallow water, most coral reefs are located near land. Fringing reefs and barrier reefs are two common types of coral reef. *Fringing Reefs* are located directly off the shores of tropical islands and continents, whereas *Barrier Reefs* are separated from the shore by narrow stretches of calm, shallow water. The largest coral reef in the world is a barrier reef. This enormous collection of coral, called the Great Barrier Reef, stretches for more than twelve hundred miles along the coast of Australia. It is the world's largest structure built by living organisms, including humans.

Fringing reef off the Palau Islands, Micronesia.

Atolls, the third major type of coral reef, are isolated rings of coral. Unlike other reefs, atolls are usually located far from land, surrounded by nothing but water. Since coral polyps cannot survive in deep water, these isolated rings of coral puzzled scientists for many years. We now know that atolls are formed over thousands of years, as volcanic islands slowly sink beneath the surface of the ocean. The coral polyps grow fast enough to keep the top layer of the reef near the ocean's surface. Given enough time, some atolls develop into islands made entirely of coral.

Coral atoll in Micronesia.

As we have learned, fringing reefs, barrier reefs, and atolls are all constructed by stony corals. Stony corals, however, are not the only type of coral found in a reef. *Soft Corals,* so named because they do not produce hard skeletons, also inhabit many reefs. Because they are not supported by hard skeletons, soft coral colonies are much smaller and more delicate than stony coral colonies. Also unlike stony corals, soft corals do not need sunlight in order to develop properly. As a result, their colonies are often found in deeper parts of a reef.

Gorgonians are another type of coral living in many reefs. Like soft corals, gorgonian polyps lack hard, outer skeletons; however, they do have flexible internal skeletons. This enables their colonies to develop long, thin branches that look like delicate fans or feathers.

Page 24: Soft coral polyps feeding.
Page 25: Gorgonia coral.

Coral polyps are not the only animals that live in coral reefs; thousands of other animals are nestled in the underwater cracks and crevices. One of the more interesting reef inhabitants is the *Tube Worm*. Tube worms do not look at all like the long, slithery worms that live on land. Many tube worms are decorated with thin tentacles that resemble flowers or delicate feather dusters. They use their tentacles to filter food from the water and to take in oxygen. Like coral polyps, tube worms withdraw into hard, rocklike shelters if they are disturbed.

Open and closed tube worms.

The *Sea Anemone*, a distant relative of the corals, is another interesting inhabitant of the reef community. Anemones are giant-sized polyps that grow up to two feet tall. Most sea anemones live alone. They attach themselves to rocks or burrow into sand on the ocean floor. The anemone's mouth, like that of a coral polyp, is surrounded by poisonous tentacles. An anemone uses its tentacles to capture small fish and to protect itself from enemies.

Crimson anemone.

For most reef inhabitants, as for the sea anemone, avoiding enemies is a full-time job. There are enemies lurking within every nook and cranny of the reef. Many reef organisms protect themselves with hard outer coverings. The *Marine Snail* hides its soft body within a hard, spiraled shell. A clam or an oyster, on the other hand, is protected by two bowl-shaped shells, which open like a treasure chest to take in tiny particles of food. Although most clams are smaller than your hand, some weigh over five hundred pounds and grow up to four feet wide.

Pink clownfish under cover.

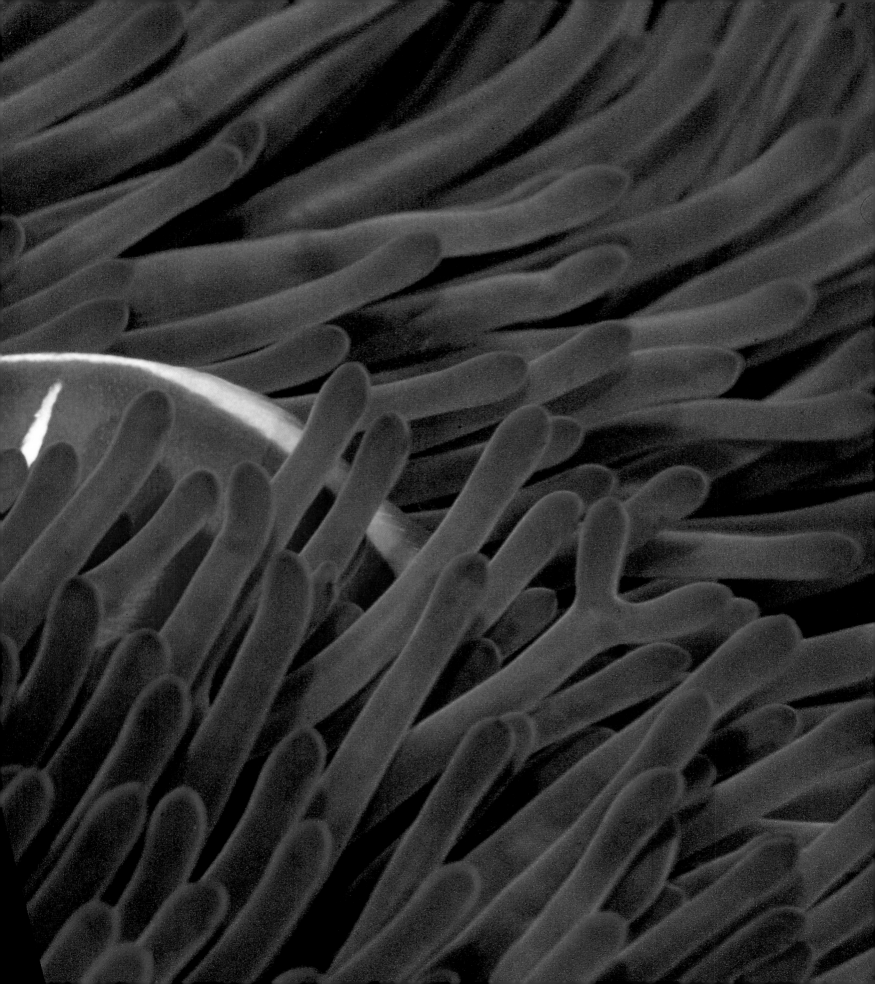

Instead of smooth, hard shells, sea stars and sea urchins are covered with tough, sharp spines. This protective armor is usually enough to discourage potential enemies. If a sea star is damaged, however, it can actually regrow lost body parts. In fact, it can grow a whole new body even if it loses four of its five arms.

In a coral reef, one of the most common ways to avoid being eaten is to avoid being detected altogether. The *Octopus* is a reef-dweller that is a master of disguise. This unusual, eight-legged animal not only changes colors, but also varies the texture of its skin to blend in with the underwater land-scape. Thus disguised, the octopus is nearly invisible and can usually avoid its enemies. If it is threatened, however, the octopus has an additional line of defense. It squirts out a thick cloud of black ink and quickly swims to safety.

Page 32: Green sea urchins.
Page 33: An Atlantic octopus hunts at night.

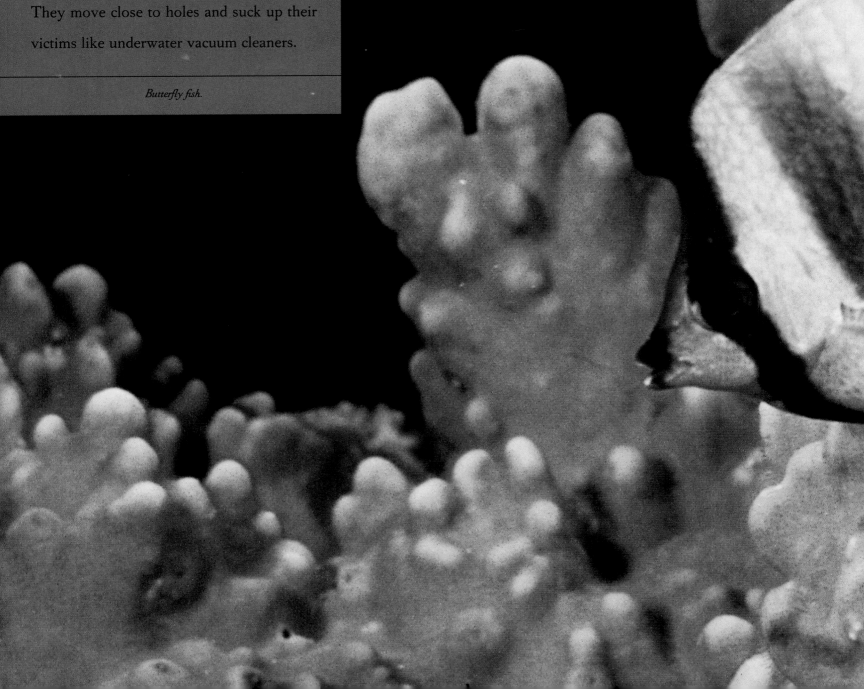

In addition to their inventive methods of protection, reef organisms also have interesting methods for finding food. *Butterfly Fish* have long snouts that they use to probe underwater cracks and crevices, where they can find tasty crabs and worms. *Nurse Sharks,* on the other hand, do not need long snouts to capture hidden morsels of food. They move close to holes and suck up their victims like underwater vacuum cleaners.

Butterfly fish.

The *Moray Eel*, another species of fish, is one of the most vicious-looking inhabitants of the coral reef. This snakelike fish hides from its victims in underwater caves. When an unsuspecting creature swims within reach, the eel lunges from its hiding place and snatches its victim in its sharp, pointed teeth.

The *Wrasse* is a reef-dwelling fish that has one of the most unusual methods of acquiring food. This fish actually provides a cleaning service for other sea creatures. Using its long, pointed snout, the wrasse removes bits of debris from other fishes' bodies. It even picks scraps of food from the teeth of sharks or eels. The arrangement works well for both parties—the wrasse gets bits of food to eat, while its customers receive a cleansing bath.

Moray eel being cleaned by a wrasse.

While many reef animals have unusual methods for obtaining food, others simply rely on strength and speed. Often referred to as the "tiger of the sea," the *Great Barracuda* is always on the prowl for another meal. Growing up to ten feet long, an adult barracuda swims quietly through warm, tropical reefs. When an appetizing meal strays within range, the barracuda strikes with lightning-quick speed. Armed with powerful jaws filled with daggerlike teeth, the barracuda devours its meal with a few quick, clean bites.

Barracuda!

Hidden beneath the Earth's tropical seas, *Coral Reefs* are enormous underwater cities. They are built by tiny coral polyps and inhabited by millions of fascinating creatures. Coral reefs are unlike anything on land. Although we are only visitors, we are fortunate to get a glimpse of these underwater worlds and their amazing collections of life.

A coral cave in the Red Sea.